Terry Gould

TRANSITION
IN THE EARLY YEARS

FEB 1 9 2013

PROPERTY OF
SENECA COLLEGE
LIBRARIES
KING CAMPUS

WITHDRAWN

D1028779

From principles into practice

Published 2012 by Featherstone Education
Bloomsbury Publishing Plc
50 Bedford Square, London,
www.acblack.com

ISBN 978-1-4081-6396-2

Text © Terry Gould 2012
Design © Lynda Murray
Photographs © Acorn Childcare and Fotolia

A CIP record for this publication is available from the British Library.
All rights reserved. No part of this publication may be reproduced
in any form or by any means – graphic, electronic, or mechanical, including
photocopying, recording, taping or information storage or retrieval systems –
without the prior permission in writing of the publishers.

Printed in Great Britain by Latimer Trend & Company Ltd

10 9 8 7 6 5 4 3 2 1

This book is produced using paper that is made from wood grown in
managed, sustainable forests. It is natural, renewable and recyclable.
The logging and manufacturing processes conform to the environmental
regulations of the country of origin.

To see our full range of titles visit **www.acblack.com**

Acknowledgements
We would like to thank the staff and children of Acorn Childcare, Milton Keynes for
their time and patience in helping put this book together, including the use of a
number of photographs.

Contents

Introduction

Whenever I talk to people about transition, everyone appears to see it as an important aspect of their practice and most have a written policy on this. However, what I often see when I visit settings is an inconsistency in the way the policy is applied. Very often this appears to be due to the induction and monitoring processes set up within the setting, which in the end comes down to the quality of self evaluation in place.

Transition affects all young children and by the time they reach school age many will already have experienced several transition periods, particularly if they have attended a full daycare setting, including:

- **the transition from home to the setting**

- **the transition between room bases in the setting**

- **the transition from a childcare provider to school**

- **and sometimes the transition from one provider to another during the working week.**

Children who are effectively and successfully supported through early transitions learn positive ways of coping with change. As they grow they are more likely to cope with change whenever it may occur and at any stage of their lives. Overall we know that most transitions that children make are successful, but for a minority of children they are not and this has negative implications for their future well-being and their capacity to enjoy and achieve in their childhood and adolescence.

This book has been written to support practitioners in helping children and their families adapt to change. The target of providing high quality early childhood experiences, including transitions, is shared by all early years practitioners. These quality experiences can occur in a range and variety of places including home, school, childminders, day nurseries, children's centres and play-groups.

As children develop from birth and right through their childhood they move from one learning environment or setting to a new one. They are therefore almost always on a journey, and permanently in transition. Often, these transitions involve a process of change that requires a period of adjustment for both the child and their family. Both children and their families need continuity of education and care and it is a requirement of the revised Early Years Foundation Stage (EYFS) (DfE 2012) that we offer this

through as much continuity and support as possible. This is accomplished when practitioners from the previous setting (senders) and the next setting (receivers) work together.

Early years settings which are most successful in handling transitions are those which make planning for transition a priority. There is no doubt that transition periods are times which can be very stressful for children, parents/carers and practitioners alike but by considering the key factors of transition, outlined in this book, it should be possible to make the move from one situation to another a positive experience for all concerned; so that it is full of excitement and anticipation rather than uncertainty and anxiety. When children move from their home to a setting, or from one setting to another they can potentially experience a lot of anxiety, including feelings of sadness and resistance.

Our role as practitioners is to make any transition as seamless as possible, so making it as far as possible, a positive experience for the child and their family. It is the child's key person and parents/carers who should take the lead in all the arrangements and events of the move.

However, all those working in the EYFS will need to be aware that children bring different experiences, interests and competencies with them, which affect their ability to learn. The transition process must therefore make extra efforts to recognise and meet the special and additional needs of individual children.

Terry Gould
May 2012

Chapter 1
Effective transition

Effective transition

> **"**
>
> *If we take a child's physical pain seriously, then we must also do the same for their emotional pain.*
>
> **Margot Sunderland (2006)**
>
> **"**

What do we really mean by effective transition? Is everyone on the team sure about being consistent but also about how to act in different situations?

One dictionary definition of transition is *'movement, passage, or change from one position, state, stage, subject, concept, etc., to another'* and this is precisely what transition is all about… CHANGE.

To try to get a better understanding in a fun way you could do a two-part exercise involving you and your team. First show them a picture of a desert island and ask them to imagine they are shipwrecked near this desert island and that they can take three personal items with them from the ship, before it is washed away. Give them little or no time to think, then ask them to write on a post-it note which three items they would choose. Collect these in and record on a large sheet of paper or flip chart.

Then show them a picture of a hotel on a beach in a very desirable location and tell them to choose up to five things they wouldn't want to be without when visiting the hotel. This time, give them a few minutes to think and talk and then again ask them to record these on post-it notes. Collect these in and record on a flip chart.

Have a discussion about the two tasks including:

- **How difficult they felt each task was**

- **How they felt during each task**

- **Which they felt was the harder or easier task and why**

- **How they might have felt in real life in these situations**

- **How each person had chosen different things and some the same**

- **How some took much longer to choose than others**

Then liken these tasks to the transition process. It's a very interesting activity to do and the choices people make can tell you a lot about that person. Hopefully, it should really support a greater level of understanding that the unforeseen is much more difficult than the foreseen for all of us to deal with, whatever our age and experience.

Let's move on now to thinking again about the setting that you work in and an overview of effective transition for children to, through and from this.

An overview of effective transition in the early years recognises that:

- **it is a process**

- **it is a journey**

- **at least one area of our life is always in transition; always moving towards the next stage**

- **at any one time, anywhere during the journey, we can look back to where we once were and anticipate what may come in the future.**

Transition as we know it for our very young children involves moving from one environment/situation to another and hence it is a continual process for them. They are almost always on a journey, and almost permanently in transition. The process of transition itself may therefore be viewed as one of adaptation. Sally Featherstone, in the book *Smooth Transitions* (2003), covering Reception to Year1, alludes to four key aspects to consider when putting research into practice: **space, time, people** and **information**.

Each of these can be used to help children and their parents/carers adapt to the changes they encounter. Research has shown that the best adaptation takes place where:

- **conditions are similar**

- **communication is encouraged**

- **the process of change takes place gradually over time.**

We know from our experience, and that of others, that transition is not a one-off event but something that happens on an ongoing basis. All staff in any EYFS team need to keep this thought at the forefront of their minds. Children may move between several different settings in the course of a day, a week, a month or a year. Points of transition are a critical time emotionally for young children and as such, need to

be planned and managed sensitively. Children's social, emotional and educational needs are central to any transition between one setting and another or within one setting. Some children and their parents/carers will find transition stressful while others will not appear to find it so. Others again may even appear to enjoy the experience, and will quickly make the move with little or no apparent stress. It is helpful if we can understand what makes transition effective and ultimately successful. With this in mind, I have identified four considerations which I shall call my four 'keys' to effective transition that open the door to success. These are:

1 🗝 **Effective consultation**

2 🗝 **Good quality communication**

3 🗝 **Continuity and consistency**

4 🗝 **Effective sharing of information**

All my experience tells me that there are always important things to consider in any important life situation that involves change. Transition is no exception and I believe that these are the four key considerations (identified above) which we need to focus upon to be effective and successful within the process of transition.

Effective consultation

The first of these keys to success is effective consultation with all the stakeholders, especially parents and carers. Although information about each child needs to be gathered through discussion, it is useful to give parents/carers a booklet for them and their child to complete together in their own time before the transition visit. This enables them to share information about their child and their family such as interests, likes, dislikes, medical needs, allergies and so on with the setting before the child starts.

Periods of change, especially for the families of babies and the very youngest children, can be made much less daunting if parents/carers are consulted and their views taken into account, understood and respected, and they feel that they have some say over what happens in any new or changing situation. Fundamental to any consultation with parent/carers is the recognition that they are their children's prime carers and first educators. In the most effective settings, practitioners understand the importance of parents/carers being involved in their child's learning and in all ways welcome their views, knowledge and opinions about their child.

Good quality communication

The second key, good quality communication, recognises that parents/carers who are effectively, purposefully and sensitively communicated with feel valued and secure in the knowledge that their individual child's needs are being catered for. Equally importantly, successful transitions from one room base to another, or from one setting to another, are dependent on parents/carers and practitioners communicating with one another and respecting, and building on, the information provided by parents/carers their colleagues and other professionals.

But what about the children who take a longer period to adapt to change? Time is the crucial factor for them if we are to aid their transition: they are likely to need plenty of time to explore and absorb their surroundings and they need time to adjust and feel comfortable with their new environment. We need to communicate with parents/carers about how their child is settling in and this is best supported by a number of visits before they start their placement and lots of informative and useful discussions with parents/carers.

Continuity and consistency

The third key to successful transition is a high degree of continuity and consistency in the approach to transition from all those involved. This requires all adults working with young children to have a clear understanding about the principles of the EYFS and those aspects that will need to be continued as the child moves through this stage and later into the next.

The four overarching principles of the revised EYFS (DfE 2012) are:

● **Every child is a unique child, who is constantly learning and can be resilient, capable, confident and self-assured.**

● **Children learn to be strong and independent through positive relationships.**

● **Children learn and develop well in enabling environments, in which their experiences respond to their individual needs and there is a strong partnership between practitioners and parents and/or carers.**

● **Children develop and learn in different ways and at different rates. The framework covers the education and care of all children in early years provision, including children with SEN and disabilities.**

All staff need to adopt a consistent approach in line with these principles, and the transition policy of the setting, that is open and transparent to all involved parties. Staff must ensure that they communicate effectively in consistent ways with parents/carers and children about transition beforehand and always include/facilitate visits wherever possible.

4

Effective sharing of information

The fourth key to successful transition is the effective sharing of information both verbally and in written format. Settings need to provide guidance for parents/carers on how they can prepare for and support their children's learning and development in the new setting including:

- **the environment changes that the child will encounter indoors and outdoors**

- **changes to routines he/she will encounter in the new setting**

- **the new staff including his/her new key person**

- **meeting some of the new children he/she will encounter**

- **any new uniform/clothing requirements**

- **taking into account the concerns of working parents/carers and children with particular needs**

- **emphasis on this for those children who have English as an additional language (EAL) or SEN (see p13-15).**

Prior to the child starting at the setting, the key person should meet with the parents/carers to share information about how the setting operates such as timings of sessions and the costs involved. He/she should also share and or find out information about the child including:

- **the important adults in the child's life**

- **the child's interests**

- **their favourite foods**

- **their sleep patterns**

- **how the child usually shows anxiety or distress**

- **what soothes/comforts him/her**

- **the child's motivation and schemas (patterns of play)**

- **how the parent/carer would like to approach the first separation.**

The staff in individual settings or schools should view transition as a 'process' rather than an event. The managers and leaders should enable staff in the EYFS to meet with staff in the next room/class to share information and discuss individual children in order to help them to plan to meet their needs.

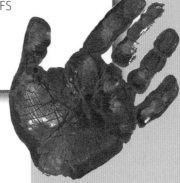

First impressions count

We must all remember that the first impression parents/carers and the young child gain is critical in helping to shape their views of the setting and what it offers. Putting the four 'keys' into practice will ensure that you can provide a positive experience so that a good first impression is provided.

First impressions do really matter and you will only get one chance to make that first impression at a point of transition. Remember that good initial first contact with parents/carers and recognition of the unique child is a key feature in beginning to build the positive relationships that are required. Parents/carers will often be anxious and may not have been in a nursery/school educational environment for some time; so a warm, welcoming and friendly atmosphere will help them to relax. It is important therefore to consider a number of things including:

- ✓ clearly signposting the entrance, office, toilet and other key areas

- ✓ providing a bright, welcoming and informative environment which reflects cultural diversity

- ✓ making sure the person who shows parents/carers round the setting is both knowledgeable and friendly

- ✓ making sure all practitioners (including administration staff) are aware of and clear about the transition process and schedule

- ✓ bearing in mind that parents/carers may be anxious about whether their children will get a place at the setting

- ✓ completing any necessary forms in partnership with the parents/carers

- ✓ providing a translator where needed

- ✓ helping parents/carers to make informed decisions about their children by giving them full information and answering their questions.

All of these measures take time and effort but it is well worth the effort when the transition experience goes well and the child settles into their new setting.

Recognising and meeting the special and additional needs of individual children

You will need to put in particular extra effort for any children recognised as having additional needs or SEN. Here the focus is on two particular groups of children:

- children whose home language is not English (EAL)

- children with SEN.

Children with EAL

Settling in is a particularly important time for EAL children and it is important for the success of this, to ensure that the environment and resources reflect in some way their family, ethnicity, religion and culture. Some languages are given lower status than others in our society and this will affect how children and adults feel about themselves, as language is very closely linked to identity and self-esteem. It is crucial that practitioners value and celebrate language diversity and recognise the importance of maintaining and developing the child's mother tongue.

EAL children and their families will often have very specific needs which practitioners need to take into account in order to help them settle into their new environment. For example:

- **Parents/carers may have had very different educational experiences from the ones we are offering. Settings may need to provide extra support to help their understanding of how and why we plan for young children to learn through play.**

- **Recent arrival families, or asylum seekers and those with refugee status, may be coping with particularly difficult social circumstances, which practitioners need to be aware of in order to support the child appropriately.**

- **Families with refugee status/asylum seekers may have had to cope with traumatic experiences and loss, which can mean they are emotionally vulnerable. Settings need to be very sensitive as families may choose not to discuss these issues with you.**

- **Children can benefit from being linked up with another child as a 'buddy'.**

- **The transition time will be very tiring for children so try to make it as easy as possible for them.**

- Ensure language is supported and enabled, making sure that access to language is embedded using visual and other stimuli.

- If all families are offered home visits, be sensitive to the fact that some families may be housed in temporary accommodation and may not want to be visited in these circumstances.

- Some children and parents/carers may speak or understand very little or no English.

- Families who arrive with very little English may experience the situation of needing to depend on others, sometimes older children, for help with interpreting until they acquire sufficient English. You need to be thoughtful as to who you ask to help with interpreting, start by asking parents/carers to identify a friend or family member they will feel comfortable with.

- Offer translating and interpreting to parents/carers so that they can access induction meetings, fill in admission forms and so on.

- As dietary rules are often an essential aspect of religious practice, ensure accurate information is gathered from families about what their child can or cannot eat.

- Develop a range of resources to support the sharing of information, for example a photo booklet about the nursery/class with the session times displayed on a clock face and your information booklet/school prospectus translated into a range of languages.

- When the child starts at the setting, ensure that accurate information is gathered about the languages a child and their family use and understand.

- Encourage parents/carers to continue to talk with their children in their mother tongue.

- Introduce parents/carers to other parents/carers who speak the same home language.

Children with SEN

It is important that the setting is ready to meet the needs of all children, including those with an identified SEN, and this will mean knowing and understanding their needs fully. It is critical that a multi-agency approach is adopted and information about children with SEN is shared with their next setting. This allows the receiving setting to build up a balanced profile on individual children, guards against vital information being missed on admission, gives the opportunity for the next setting to provide any necessary resources and equipment and provides the chance to liaise with other professionals.

Strategies to employ include:

➜ Meetings should be arranged with SEN co-ordinators (SENCOs) from both the sending provision and the receiving setting to discuss the child's individual needs **providing a transitional review**. This provides the opportunity to share information between all staff involved and helps to prepare fully for the comprehensive integration of the child into the setting, including any further strategies necessary to support the individual needs of the child and those of their parent/carer. This will substantially help to make the transition as smooth as possible.

➜ Extra/additional transition visits should be planned, on a needs-led basis, to enable the children and parents/carers to familiarise themselves with the new setting and its routines and for the child to be observed in their responses to the new provision. These events should take place when the setting is operating and children are in situ and should be arranged when staff have time to devote to the child and parents/carers.

➜ All information and records (such as statements, medical history, Individual Education Plans, reports from other agencies, medical information and information provided by the parents/carers) must be handed over to the receiving setting in good time and before the child makes any visits to the new setting. Further meetings should be arranged to clarify/confirm information concerning the child, as appropriate.

➜ In the case of a transition from home to a setting, liaise with professionals from any pre-school special needs services and/or other agencies who have vital additional information on the child or insight into their needs.

➜ Ensure consent from the parent/carer is obtained before information is passed to the receiving setting.

➜ When reviewing policy and practice on transition, it is useful to check if all the above are maintained within your setting's policy.

Chapter 2
The stages of transition

The stages of transition

> **"**
> We can never remind ourselves too often that a child, particularly a very young and almost totally dependent one, is the only person in the nursery who cannot understand why he/she is there
>
> **Goldschmied and Jackson (1994)**
> **"**

There is a vast amount of potential for very young children to become overwhelmed and bewildered as they start at a daycare/school setting for the first time. They find themselves being parted from the people with whom they have bonded and find it incredibly difficult, if not impossible at first, to understand the reasons why. It is therefore most helpful if the setting ensures that sufficient time is allocated to the settling in period: explaining the transition process to parents/carers, providing the right climate for gradual separation, at a pace appropriate for the individuals concerned, recognising that for individual children the time required will be different; some will need more others less. The more that all staff and parents/carers understand the stages that children will go through the better. Some children will spend longer at some stages than others and this is important to bear in mind. For example, those children who do not settle for a very long time often remain at the 'trying to let go' stage, for much longer than most other children.

The three main stages

There are three main stages of transition which all staff need to know about and understand so that they can plan and prepare children to go through them.

These are:

1 **The trying to let go stage**

2 The being uncertain stage

3 The taking hold stage

1

The trying to let go stage

As children prepare to leave a familiar setting or situation they will go through feelings of sadness and resistance to the change. This often leads to them being confused and/or overwhelmed and as a consequence they may revert to previous behaviours.

● **Temper tantrums/lack of self control.**
As adults we can recognise and feel the strong emotions brought on by separation and being away from our families, but we need the rational understanding to know that our survival is not automatically threatened by it. Saying that parents or carers are coming back soon will come to mean something eventually, but at this point of time in the transition process it is of little help to a young child whose brain cannot yet process that type of information with any true sense of meaning.

● **Appearing to be fussy or whiney.**
It is vital that children have their tears, fears and other feelings acknowledged, and accepted. This is an important part of the transition process for the child, and extremely valuable for their emotional health and well-being in the longer term. What these children do not need at this stage is a practitioner/key person who tells them they don't need to be sad or miserable or uses distraction methods to try to lessen their feeling of anxiety or distress.

● **Crying easily, perhaps for no understandable reason.**
A child who cries when separated from their primary attachment figure of mum or dad or another family member is just doing what comes naturally, from their perspective they are crying for very good reasons. The human baby/infant brain has a strong instinct for survival, and to a young child dependent on the proximity of a parent/carer for their survival, separation can pose the very serious threat of being left and abandoned. The brain triggers a distress response and as a result the child does what comes naturally and cries, because this is the most effective way he/she has of communicating their feelings of distress.

● **Re-emergence of habits that they appeared to have outgrown e.g. thumb sucking.**
The first major transitions from home and family, into care or education outside the home, all take place at a time when children's brains are instinctively programmed to actively resist that separation.

2

The being uncertain stage

- At this stage children are often confused about what will happen next and this heightens their feelings of worry and/or fear.
  The separation distress system in a young child's brain is hypersensitive and constantly on the alert for the threat of abandonment and anything that might threaten the child's survival. They feel unsure about what will happen next and they need a friendly face to turn to for assurance.

- It is important that children have visited the new setting and learned about the routines there before they start.
  Those children who have made several visits are likely to feel much less uncertain than those who have not. It is most important that daily transitions are handled sensitively. Young children may be tired as well as relieved to see their parent/carer and in turn parents/carers need to understand that because their child cries when they see them does not mean the child has had a bad day. It is just a stage they are going through.

- Adults need to try to be clear with children about the things that are changing or different and to answer any questions that children raise.
  As practitioners, we have to check in with our own feelings when we respond to the distress of a child or a parent/carer struggling with separation. Their distress can trigger anxieties of our own, such as concerns about how we are going to handle an agitated, screaming child along with all our other responsibilities first thing in the morning. Being clear about the routine of the day and things that are different are important to reassure the child about. For example, if their key person is not going to be at the setting we need to alert both the child and the parent/carer and explain who will be their first point of support and contact on arrival and during the day.

- It is good practice to allow the children to bring a familiar toy or object from the previous setting or from home with them.
  The important three-way relationship between parent/carer, child and key person will be built gradually, over time and in a variety of ways. Links with home during the day, through a toy or familiar object, can help to alleviate some of the child's worries and can act as a comforter to reassure them.

3

The taking hold stage

- Children at this stage need supportive and encouraging guidance on what is expected of them as well as affirmation that they are acting appropriately. This should include lots of praise, smiles and positive eye contact. Both the child and the parent/carer can benefit from the presence of a sensitive practitioner to soothe and understand their anxieties and concerns.

- Practitioners can help children settle and gain confidence at this stage by:

  - **making new routines explicit**

  - **reviewing expectations**

  - **pointing out to children what they are learning.**

As Goldschmied and Jackson (1994) point out, practitioners need to ensure that they acknowledge and accept their own feelings of anxiety when settling children, by sharing their personal feelings with colleagues and supervisors.

Getting in touch with our own feelings helps us to appreciate the feelings of the children and parents/carers we work with, making us better able to support them through the challenge of daily transitions. We need to consider everything from the child's perspective and respond appropriately to how we observe they are feeling.

Chapter 3

The key person and transition

The key person and transition

> " Each child must be assigned a key person. Their role is to help ensure that every child's care is tailored to meet their individual needs to help the child become familiar with the setting, offer a settled relationship for the child and build a relationship with their parents.
>
> **DfE (2012)** "

The role of the key person should ensure that parents/carers are able to talk to a specific member of staff to ensure that their child is being cared for appropriately and their needs met. In their key person, children will have a specific person at the setting for them to bond with and someone they know will advocate for them.

This is particularly important at times of transition within each setting, between different settings which a child attends in any one week and during the transition between an early years setting and school. The key person will take on the role of providing parents/carers with the information they need including practical information about the setting such as session times, clothes, food and how best to take up the opportunities to:

- **visit and become familiar with the new room/setting**

- **get to know practitioners particularly their child's new key person**

- **meet and get to know other parents/ carers**

- **share information about their child and family.**

Peter Elfer, Elinor Goldschmied and Dorothy Selleck (2011) describe home/setting relationships as a 'triangle of trust' between the child, their family and the key people in the school or setting and this starts when the child first arrives to visit.

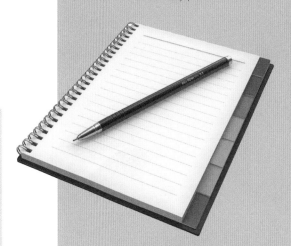

> "The key person approach has a powerful part to play in supporting these daily transitions. Sensitive and responsive 'handover rituals' support and reassure both child and parent as well as providing time and space for informal chats and sharing of information.'
>
> **Anne O'Connor (2008)**

Supporting transition is an integral part of the key person role and can include:

- carrying out home visits or one-to-one meetings to gather information about children and their families

- carrying out the necessary preparations prior to new children starting at the setting/school such as making coat peg/milk labels, setting up individual storage areas, providing a change of clothes and so on

- supporting the children and their parents/carers through the gradual admission process for example, compiling case notes, discussing the setting's policies, procedures, organisation, introducing other staff and so on

- establishing and maintaining positive and effective relationships with the children, their parents/carers and wider family such as sharing information about their children's likes and dislikes

- being the first point of contact for the children, their parents/carers and wider family and communicating any necessary information on a day-to-day basis

- liaising with other agencies and professionals and the setting's SENCO if individual key group children have identified additional needs

- preparing records, reports and other relevant information at the point of transition.

Supervision and peer support can greatly support the role when times are challenging and the transition is a difficult one for the parent/carer and the child. We need to ensure that we meet all the legal/data protection requirements in passing on the information regarding issues such as child protection, SEN and looked after children.

It can be a time to celebrate children's growth and achievements. This is a form of closure and it is an ideal time to review old pictures, pointing out new accomplishments and generally celebrating this phase of 'growing up'. It is vital that adults try to be clear about the things that are changing by answering any questions children may have, for example:

- **will I see my old friends again?**

- **who will be my key person or teacher?**

- **where will I have my dinner?**

- **where are the toilets?**

- **where will I play?**

- **how will I get home?**

The feelings and views of parents/carers

Developing a close working relationship with parents/carers is often crucial to a positive transition experience for the children, the families and the setting. It is vital that settings take into account the feelings and views of individual parents/carers, and make every effort to reassure them. At times of transition the needs of the children are central. However, it is easy to forget that the transition experience is also happening to parents/carers.

Some parents/carers will be very positive and confident about supporting their children through transition and working in partnership with settings/schools. They will confidently approach practitioners to ask questions, access information and clarify transition arrangements. However, many parents/carers, like their children, feel anxious about changes and new situations. They may compare or reflect on their previous transition experiences which could have been negative and may expect their children's experiences to be similar. They also have to adjust to a period of change, 'let go' of their child and entrust them to a new environment.

Chapter 4
Key research information

Key research information

Ten important key facts derived from research about transition and some implications for effective practice

The following ten facts have been extracted from research into good practice in the transition process. These facts can be helpful for staff teams in recognising how well they match up to some of the findings. Whilst each fact has an implication identified in the book, in practice this could also be expanded upon by the staff as a whole team and more implications identified.

Fact 1

By the time they reach school age many children will already have experienced several transition periods, particularly if they have attended a full daycare setting, including: the transition from home to the setting; the transition between room bases; the transition from a childcare provider to school; possibly, the transition from one provider to another during the working week.

Implications for practice

Transition in not an event and must be treated as a process that is ongoing.

Fact 2

Early years settings which are most successful in handling transitions are those which make planning for transition a priority. There is no doubt that transition periods are times which can be stressful for children, parents/carers and practitioners alike.

Implications for practice

Always put the children's social and emotional well-being at the centre of the transition process.

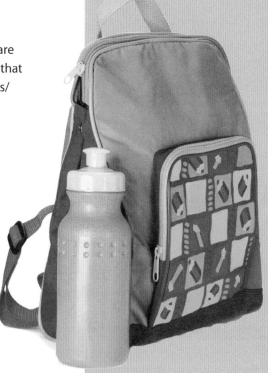

Fact 3

By considering and responding to specific factors derived from research, it should be possible to make the move from one situation to another a positive time for all concerned. This should help to create an experience which is full of excitement and anticipation rather than uncertainty and anxiety.

Implications for practice

All staff need appropriate training on transition and to understand the transition policy of the setting.

Fact 4

A key to the success of transition is effective consultation with all the stakeholders, especially parents and carers. Periods of change, especially for the families of the very youngest children, can be made less daunting if parents/carers' views are respected and they feel that they have some say over what happens in new situations.

Implications for practice

Make sure that sufficient time is allocated for consultation with parents/carers and children and the receiving setting staff.

Fact 5

Equally important is that successful transitions from one room base to another, or from one setting to another, are dependent on practitioners consulting one another and respecting and building on, the information provided by their colleagues.

Implications for practice

Have clear and transparent guidelines set within your policy and ensure all staff have an induction period when this is highlighted.

Fact 6

Consulting in appropriate ways with children on what makes transitions easier and more enjoyable for them, will help to determine the setting's policy on transition. Providing time for staff to observe children in their previous room or setting will give the receiving practitioners the opportunity to note children's individual interests and areas in which they may need support.

Implications for practice

Children are able to consult in a range of ways on their transition according to the stage of their development and we should identify the most effective ways of doing this. Ensuring enough time is allocated for the child to make visits to the new setting is very important.

Fact 7

One of the major barriers to parental involvement in early years settings identified in the *Parents as Partners in Early Learning* (PPEL) report was ineffective communication. Smooth transitions are dependent on settings providing as much information as possible on policies, organisation, routines, personnel and pedagogy. While there will be information which each setting feels it wishes to impart to parents/carers, it is useful to carry out an informal survey to find out what it is that parents/carers actually want to know, particularly about transition. Information can then be presented in a way that is useful to parents/carers and practitioners. It is essential that information is easily understood, jargon free and produced in a range of languages as appropriate.

Implications for practice

Settings which prioritise, giving staff time to talk to parents/carers each day will be able to minimise concerns about change. Some parents/carers prefer to speak directly to staff at the beginning or end of the day; others may prefer written information which they can take home to read. The sorts of information provided for parents/carers will vary with the age of the child. Opportunities should be provided for parents/carers to meet with staff if there is anything they do not understand or which they may not agree with.

Fact 8

Continuity for children and their families is crucial in making successful transitions. Settings which invest time in planning for continuity will benefit from having secure, happy children and relaxed and interested parents/carers. As a result, staff will feel confident that they are able to cope with the social, emotional and educational needs of the children in their care. Well established routines will provide the framework for continuity in any setting. An element of predictability in daily routines provides security for children and gives them a feeling of self-confidence in knowing what will happen next.

Implications for practice

Children need to be shown things that are the same or broadly similar and those which are new/different, in the environment and routines, and they will need the reasons for this explained to them.

Fact 9

Consistency in staff attitudes is essential if children and their parents/carers are not to be confused about what is expected or acceptable. This is particularly important in terms of acceptable behaviour, how it will be encouraged and how unacceptable behaviour will be addressed. Settings may find that their acceptable standards of behaviour are not entirely consistent with those of individual families.

Implications for practice

Practitioners will need to know exactly how to deal with any difficult situations when they occur. Updated staff training on transition should be undertaken at least once a year and as situations require this.

Fact 10

Settling-in procedures should be flexible, allowing time for individual children and their parents/carers to be comfortable with the change in their lives. For many children, reminders of home are crucially important and settings should include opportunities for children to talk about their family members, perhaps by introducing things like 'family books' or a 'memory box'.

Implications for practice

Recognition of the importance of the flexibility of the transition process should be a key part of the staff induction process and updated training for all staff as a team.

Chapter 5
Principles and good practice indicators

Transition principles and good practice indicators

> People will forget what you say, people will forget what you do, but they will never forget how you made them feel.
>
> **Anonymous**

This chapter details ten key principles which fundamentally underpin effective transition practice for young children in the EYFS and beyond into Year 1. It will also provide useful details of essential and desirable ways of putting these into practice that can be observed, monitored and recorded and which are referred to as 'indicators of good practice'.

★ Principle 1

Transition is regarded by all involved as **a process and not an event**. It does not only take place during a specific week, on a specific day, at the end of the summer term or the end of the autumn term.

★ Principle 2

All adults* involved in the transition process should be **well informed and have a clear understanding of the transition process**.

★ Principle 3

Information passed on during the transition process should **take account of as many positives as possible** so that children can build on their successes early in their new surroundings.

★ Principle 4

Building positive relationships with parents/carers and working in partnership with them is crucial to the success of the transition process as it ensures that children's individual needs are met.

(*this will include parents, carers and practitioners).

Principle 5

Communication, flexibility and organisation are the keys to a smooth and effective transition process.

 Principle 6

Partnership with other professionals forms an integral part of successful transition processes and helps to ensure that the wide ranging needs of both children and parents/carers are met appropriately.

 Principle 7

Multi-agency working ensures the sharing of information and lessens the chances of vital information being omitted during the transitional period.

 Principle 8

Transition should be handled sensitively and thoughtfully, always with the **children's social, emotional and educational needs central to the process**.

 Principle 9

Effective transition procedures are based on **an inclusive policy** which complies with the requirements of the EYFS and other Local Authority (LA) guidance.

 Principle 10

Transition should involve **consultation with children** at a level appropriate to their needs and stage of development allowing them to express their ideas and thoughts.

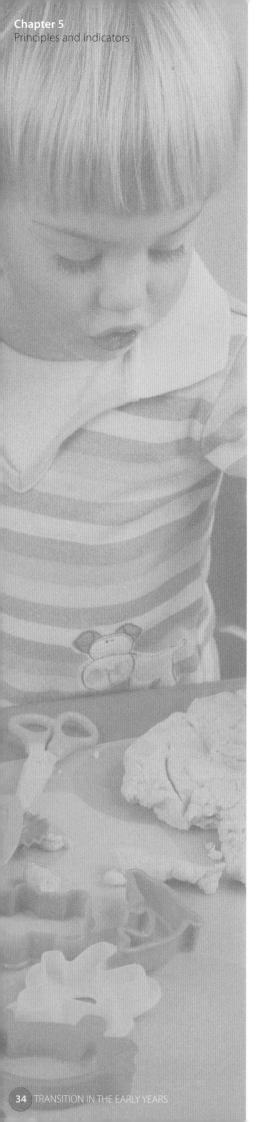

★ Principle 1

Transition is regarded by all involved as a process and not an event. It does not only take place during a specific week, on a specific day, at the end of the summer term or the end of the autumn term.

Indicators of good practice:

Essential

- ✓ Use 'all about me' type of information gathering format from parents/carers

- ✓ Gradual admission process in place

- ✓ Progress development meetings with parents/carers and key person, formal and informal

- ✓ Staff training provided including induction for new staff

- ✓ Good initial and ongoing communication in place both verbal and written e.g. copy of policy

- ✓ Policy is clear, user-friendly and up to date

- ✓ Visit/s to setting by child and parents/carers before starting

- ✓ Information obtained from previous setting if any attended e.g. childminder

Desirable

- ★ Observation visit by key person to home and/or previous setting

- ★ Informal coffee mornings with parents/carers/key person

- ★ Transition display with policy, visual images, DVD clips perhaps around 'principles into practice'

- ★ Use of technology such as text messaging/email communication (with parental consent)

- ★ Home/ setting communication book

- ★ Use of throw away cameras at home – make book 'about me' at home

- ★ Special transition box – thinking and feelings

- ★ Transition basket

- ★ Work in partnership basket – laminated images relating to day-to-day provision/routines

★ Principle 2

All adults* involved in the transition process should be well informed and have a clear understanding of the transition process .

Indicators of good practice:

Essential

- ✓ Progress development meetings with parents/carers and key person, formal and informal

- ✓ Staff training provided including induction for new staff

- ✓ Staff fully aware that for some children and parents/carers it can be a traumatic time

- ✓ Good initial and ongoing communication in place both verbal and written e.g. information leaflets, copy of policy

- ✓ Policy is clear, user-friendly and up to date

- ✓ Policy reviewed every one to two years by staff team and parents/carers invited to contribute to this

- ✓ Arranged parents/carers meetings take place

- ✓ Visit/s to setting by child and parents/ carers before starting

- ✓ Information obtained from previous setting if any attended e.g. childminder

- ✓ Sufficient time and priority is given by the settings management to transition arrangements

Desirable

- ★ Observation visit by key person to home and/or previous setting

- ★ Informal coffee mornings with parents/carers/key person

- ★ Transition display with policy, visual images, DVD clips perhaps around 'principles into practice'

- ★ Home/setting communication book

- ★ Work in partnership basket – laminated images relating to day-to-day provision/routines

- ★ Newsletters e.g form completion needed to secure primary school place

(* this will include parents, carers and practitioners)

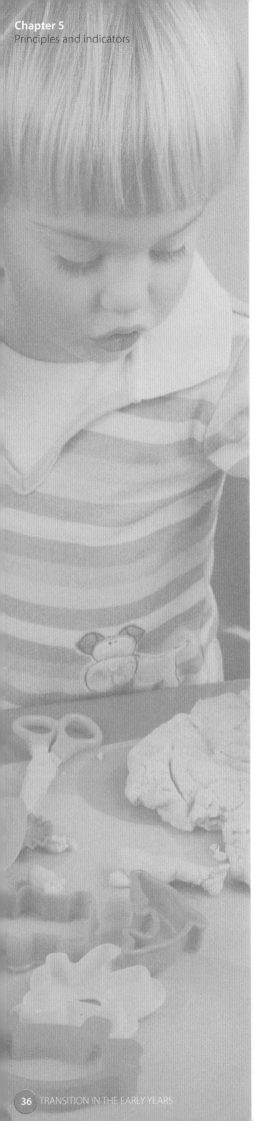

★ Principle 3

Information passed on during the transition process should take account of as many positives as possible so that children can build on their successes early in their new surroundings.

Indicators of good practice:

Essential
✓ Good initial and ongoing communication in place
✓ Communication is positive and involves lots of one-to-one talk/ discussion as well as written information being provided
✓ Staff training provided including induction for new staff
✓ Policy is clear, user-friendly, up to date and readily available
✓ Staff are supported in their understanding and examples are provided of effective transition information summaries e.g. use of words such as 'fun loving'
✓ Staff focus on what children can do best e.g. feeding themselves (under threes) or count up to ten objects accurately (three to fives) – indicating next steps for the child
✓ Appropriate updated records of children's development (learning journeys) and achievements are kept which reflect a positive view of the child
✓ As appropriate allow comforters/favourite toys and only wean off these as development occurs
✓ Sufficient time and priority is given by the settings management to transition records
✓ Management review and support any transition reports/ information and sent to the review setting

Desirable
★ A transition display is in place with policy, visual images, DVD clips perhaps around 'principles into practice'
★ Nursery books made with photos of the children are used
★ Provide mentor for new/developing staff for this aspect
★ Staff visit receiver settings on regular basis to share information to build up and maintain the relationships
★ Receiver setting staff are invited to visit the sending setting to share information and to build up and maintain the relationships

 **Principle 4**

Building positive relationships with parents/carers and working in partnership with them is crucial to the success of the transition process as it ensures that their individual needs are met.

Indicators of good practice:

Essential

- ✓ Good initial and ongoing communication in place. Communication is positive and involves lots of one-to-one talk/discussion as well as written information being provided

- ✓ Staff training provided including induction for new staff

- ✓ Policy is clear, user-friendly, up to date and readily available

- ✓ Build up trust by: (i) open and honest interactions (ii) positive body language (iii) sharing information positively (iv) being non judgemental: taking people as we find them (v) having an open-minded attitude (vi) having a policy on parent/carer partnership (vii) high quality observation strategies

- ✓ Staff supported in their understanding and examples provided of effective transition information summaries

- ✓ Appropriate updated records of children's development (learning journeys) and achievements are kept which reflect a positive view of the child

- ✓ Sufficient time and priority is given by the settings management to transition records

- ✓ Management overview transition reports/information sent to new setting

Desirable

- ★ Transition display with policy, visual images, DVD clips perhaps around 'principles into practice'

- ★ Coffee mornings for parents/carers with their child's key person

- ★ Parents/carers involved in transition policy formulation/review

- ★ Open /fun days

★ **Principle 5**

Communication, flexibility and organisation are the keys to a smooth and effective transition process.

Indicators of good practice:

Essential

✓ Good initial and ongoing communication in place. Communication is positive and involves lots of one-to-one talk/discussion as well as written information being provided

✓ Good quality observation strategies in place

✓ Staff training provided including induction for new staff enabling all to respond flexibly to children's needs and interests

✓ Consistent but flexible approach from all staff

✓ Staff make efforts to get the child's point of view/perspective

✓ Setting is ready for children by: (i) key person sorted in advance (ii) intake of children planned as staggered (iii) room information is provided verbally and in written format (iv) children's photograph on peg and in key person display

✓ Policy is clear, user-friendly, up to date and readily available

✓ Staff supported in their understanding and examples provided of effective transition information summaries e.g. use of words such as 'fun loving'

✓ Staff focus on what children can do best e.g. feeding themselves (under threes) or count up to ten objects accurately (three to fives) – indicating next steps for the child

✓ Appropriate updated records of children's development (learning journeys) and achievements are kept which reflect a positive view of the child

✓ As appropriate, allow comforters/favourite toys and only wean off these as development occurs

✓ Sufficient time and priority is given by the setting's management to transition records

✓ Management overview transition reports/information sent to new setting

Desirable

★ Transition display with policy, visual images, DVD clips perhaps around 'principles into practice'

★ All staff have professional and visible name badges

★ Staff photographs and names are prominently displayed

★ Activities are set up to engage specific children on arrival

★ Use is made of technology to support good communication e.g. text messaging and emails, with parental consent

Principle 6

Partnership with other professionals forms an integral part of a successful transition processes and helps to ensure that the wide ranging needs of both children and parents/carers are met appropriately.

Indicators of good practice:

Essential

- ✓ Decide who the other professionals are (e.g. senior leadership team, educational psychologist, social worker, LA school admissions team, other practitioners at receiving setting/room, LA parent-partnership officer etc) and decide on actions taken at transition stage and include in policy

- ✓ Good quality observation strategies in place

- ✓ Staff training provided including induction for new staff enabling all to respond flexibly to children's needs and interests

- ✓ Provide and expect good quality written information

- ✓ Consistent approach from all staff

- ✓ Staff make efforts to get the child's point of view/ perspective

- ✓ Setting is ready for children by: (i) key person sorted out in advance (ii) intake of children planned as staggered (iii) room information is provided verbally and in written format (iv) children's photograph on peg and in key person display

- ✓ Policy is clear, user-friendly, up to date and readily available

- ✓ Staff supported in their understanding and examples provided of effective transition information summaries e.g. use of words such as 'fun loving'

- ✓ SEN policy and effective practice in place

- ✓ Good records are kept

- ✓ Staff focus on what children can do best e.g. feeding themselves (under threes), or count up to ten objects accurately (three to fives) – indicating next steps for the child

- ✓ Appropriate updated records of children's development (learning journeys) and achievements are kept which reflect a positive view of the child

- ✓ As appropriate, allow comforters/ favourite toys and only wean off these as development occurs

- ✓ Sufficient time and priority is given by the settings management to transition records

- ✓ Management overview transition reports/ information sent to new setting

Desirable

- ★ List of telephone numbers, emails and addresses of other professionals, informal meetings with other professionals

- ★ Working transition lunch with receiving setting

- ★ Utilise parent-partnership officer to support parents/ carers

 Principle 7

Multi-agency working ensures the sharing of information and lessens the chances of vital information being omitted during the transitional period.

Indicators of good practice:

Essential

- ✓ Ensure that appropriate agencies are always involved in meetings to plan for the child

- ✓ Information is always provided in written form as quickly as possible after meetings

- ✓ Staff training provided including induction for new staff enabling all to respond effectively to multi-agency working

- ✓ Ensure all reports are sent out and received and necessary actions identified

- ✓ Identify who else needs a copy e.g. absent father with parental rights

- ✓ Consistent approach from all staff

- ✓ Ensure that meetings are set up well in advance so that where possible all other agencies can attend and contribute

- ✓ Parents/carers are invited to multi-agency reviews and supported to attend

- ✓ Good communication channels are established including dates confirmed by email or letter to all involved

- ✓ SENCO supports all staff

- ✓ Good records are kept e.g. SEN file

- ✓ SEN policy and effective practice in place

Desirable

- ★ List of telephone numbers, e-mails and addresses of other agencies

- ★ All staff given training in SEN work with children

 Principle 8

Transition should be handled sensitively and thoughtfully, always with the children's social, emotional and educational needs central to the process.

Indicators of good practice:

Essential

✓ Staff training provided on attitudes and including induction for new staff enabling all to respond effectively and appropriately considering language used leading to a consistent approach in place from all staff

✓ Share learning journey with new providers

✓ Good records (including learning journeys) are kept on all children – ideally managed by the key person

✓ Good observation strategies underpin practice

✓ Setting gives appropriate time and priority to transition – including allowing key person time to talk with parents/carers away from setting and answer any concerns/worries

✓ Appropriate use of 'all about me' type booklets

Desirable

★ Specific time set aside to ensure transition runs smoothly

★ Manager has one-to-one with key persons to discuss each child's individual settling in on regular basis

★ Parents/carers views on their child's transition is sought

 Principle 9

Effective transition procedures are based on an inclusive policy which complies with the requirements of the EYFS and other LA guidance.

Indicators of good practice:

Essential
✓ Staff provided with copies of any LA/national guidance are supported in using this to improve practice including putting principles into practice
✓ Staff treat the children equally but differentiate to meet each child's unique needs and interests and their cultural and religious backgrounds as appropriate
✓ Transition arrangements which are inclusive and transparent and are written in user friendly language
✓ Steps are taken to overcome barriers to admitting and providing for children with a range of physical, medical, behavioural and learning needs. Including identifying any adaptations/alterations which may be required
✓ Complies with local admission guidelines these are displayed prominently/publically in written format
✓ Practice and policy complies with SEN code of practice
✓ Practice and policy complies with 1989 Children Act, EYFS statutory guidelines

Desirable
★ Transition display
★ Appropriate use of 'all about me' type booklets

★ Principle 10

Transition should involve consultation with children at a level appropriate to their needs and stage of development allowing them to express their ideas, thoughts and emotions.

Indicators of good practice:

Essential

- ✓ Staff training provided and induction for new staff – including training on adult interactions with children and promotion of sustained shared thinking

- ✓ Children's learning journeys contain six to eight week observational-based summaries which include child's voice – can be variety of forms: photo, what child says, drawing etc

- ✓ Children ideas solicited and taken on board through a range of strategies including one-to-one discussion/talk sessions and group sessions e.g. mind-mapping

- ✓ Parents/carers asked for child's voice where children unable to provide this or as an additional tool

- ✓ Children supported to discuss their visits to new setting/room prior to their move – may draw picture or take photograph as part of the process

Desirable

- ★ Transition display

- ★ Appropriate use of 'all about me' type booklets

Chapter 6

Towards a consistent approach to transition

Towards a consistent approach to transition

It is essential that each setting/school has a policy to underpin the transition process. The transition policy should have a direct impact upon practice in each setting.

As each setting/school is unique, there is no 'one size fits all'. The policy must be placed within the whole setting/school ethos and reflect the aims of the setting.

It is useful to start with a statement that reflects the current stage of development regarding the transition plans and procedures already in place at the setting.

A policy should include sections on:

- **aims of the policy**

- **implementation of the policy**

- **monitoring of the policy**

- **evaluation of the policy.**

Creating and reviewing a transition policy

Things to consider:

- good communication systems in place
- transition policy is clear and easily accessible
- key person role is strong and effective
- home visiting takes place
- 'all about me' type booklet used with parent/carers
- gradual admission takes place

- established links have been set up between settings
- sensitivity of staff to the needs of child and parents/carers
- inclusivity of the provision environment
- information sharing meetings take place
- in-depth knowledge of SEN code of practice by staff as a team.

Strategies to consider around transition work in settings (both sender and receiver setting)

★ Work on a one to one basis to establish feelings of trust and respect with parents and children.

★ Treat children as individuals to ensure each child have equality of opportunity.

★ Find out about the child's ethnicity, faith and cultural heritage and home experiences, so that familiar experiences and interests can be used as starting points for learning and teaching.

★ Promote self-confidence and positive attitude to learning in all children, whatever their gender, ethnicity, home language, special educational needs, disability or ability.

★ Recognise that being successful and feeling confident and secure are major factors in protecting children against failure.

★ Inform parents of the value of a two-way flow of information, knowledge and expertise.

★ Ensure all parents are made to feel welcome and valued.

★ Liaise with nursery or provider/previous setting – visits by staff to meet children and parents, and by children and parents to the new setting.

★ Create an appropriate environment for good communication with parent/carers, for example, information displayed about the settings, photographs and explanations of children playing in different areas of provision.

★ Involve parents/carers in the process of induction – provide a parent's pack to include information on staff, policies and daily routines.

★ Send parents/carers regular newsletters.

★ Invite parents/carers to story sessions, lunches and events.

★ Be aware of and support parental needs, for example, literacy difficulties, English as an additional language (EAL) and special educational needs (SEN)

★ Send photographs of the staff/setting home, prior to children starting, to help familiarise them with the setting.

★ Develop flexible settling strategies, for example, building up the number of sessions the child attends in one week.

★ Collect information to support initial interests – be adaptable and flexible in your approach to the curriculum to build on children's interests – observe young children and use this to identify next steps.

★ Talk with other professionals who know the children.

★ Add a section to the prospectus that contains questions commonly asked by parents/children with appropriate responses.

★ Make the provision fun for children – show you enjoy being with them and that you value/respect them – support the building of their self-esteem and confidence.

★ Pass on information about children's progress to the next setting e.g. records and summative assessments. Settings should use this information to inform their planning.

★ Arrange welcome meetings – make parents/carers aware of the revised EYFS framework.

Bibliography and further reading

Books

Brooker, Liz (2008) *Supporting Transitions in the Early Years*
Open University Press

Elfe,r Peter, Goldschmied Elinor and Selleck Dorothy (2011)
Key Persons in the Early Years Routledge

Featherstone, Sally (2009) *Smooth Transitions: Ensuring
Continuity from the Foundation Stage* Featherstone Press

Goldschmied, Elinor, and Jackson Sonia (1994, second
edition 2003) *People Under Three: Young Children in Day Care*
Routledge

Gould, Terry (2012) *Learning and Playing Indoors* Featherstone

Statutory Framework for the Early Years Foundation Stage
(2012) Department for Education

Sunderland, Margot (2008) *The Science of Parenting*
Dorling Kindersley

Magazine articles

Bryce-Clegg, Alistair (June 2009) 'Effective Transitions:
Moving into Key Stage 1' in Early Years Educator magazine

O'Connor, Anne (March 2008) Positive relationships:
Key people - part 1 in Nursery World magazine

Tassoni, Penny (March 2012) Positive Relationships:
Behaviour – Hard to Part in Nursery World magazine

PROPERTY OF
SENECA COLLEGE
LIBRARIES
KING CAMPUS